Richard Scarry's
What Do People Do All Day?

written and illustrated by
Richard Scarry

a poet writing poems

an artist painting a picture · a story writer

a pretty model · a businessman

a photographer · a secretary · an operator

CAFE

THE NEWS

ABC

THE REMARKABLE BOOK SHOP
E. KRAMER, PROP.

a book printer · a newspaper editor

a saleslady

a newspaper reporter

a janitor

Collins
Glasgow and London

FINISH YOUR MEALS!

Wrong Way Roger

chimney sweep

dentist

doctor

eye doctor

dressmaker

beautyparlour

real estate office

music teacher

DANCING SCHOOL

BANK

CHEMIST

PRESCRIPTIONS

street cleaner

Some workers work indoors and some work outdoors. Some work up in the sky and some work underground.

water hydrant

manhole cover

manhole

wire cable

sewer

BUS STOP

lamppost

sewage pipe

TO SEWAGE PLANT

All kinds of pipes and wires are buried underground

a stuck truck

a sleeping fireman

FIRE STATION

RITZ MANSIONS

HARDWARE

window washer

BARBER SHOP

laundress

delivery boy

MOTOR CARS

car salesman

Some workers always do their work at the same place.

TELEPHONE BOOTH

Others travel from place to place to do their jobs.

What does your Daddy do?
What does your Mummy do?

jack hammer

TAXI

ditch digger

And what do YOU do?
Are you a good helper?

5

Everyone is a worker

Farmer Alfalfa   Blacksmith Fox   Stitches the tailor   Grocer Cat   Mummy   Huckle

How many workers are there here?
One, two, three, four, five, six.
What do these workers do?

Hi Daddy!

Farmer Alfalfa grows all kinds of food.
He keeps some of it for his family.

He sells the rest to Grocer Cat
in exchange for money.
Grocer Cat will sell the food
to other people in Busytown.

GROCERIES

Potatoes

Today Alfalfa bought a new suit
with some of the money he got
from Grocer Cat.
Stitches, the tailor, makes clothes.
Alfalfa bought his new suit from Stitches.

Then Alfalfa went to Blacksmith Fox's
shop. He had saved enough money
to buy a new tractor. The new tractor
will make his farm work easier.
With it he will be able to grow
more food than he could grow before.
He also bought some presents for
Mummy and his son, Alfred.

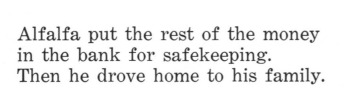

Alfalfa put the rest of the money
in the bank for safekeeping.
Then he drove home to his family.

Mummy loved her new earrings.
Alfred loved his present, too.

What did the other workers do
with the money they earned?

First they bought food to eat
and clothes to wear.
Then, they put some of the money
in the bank. Later they will use
the money in the bank
to buy other things.

What else did they buy?

Stitches bought an egg beater
so that his family could make fudge.
Try not to get any on your new clothes!

How do I look?

iron

sand
bag

bellows

forge

Blacksmith Fox bought more iron
for his shop.
He will heat and bend the metal
to make more tractors and tools.

Grocer Cat bought a new dress for Mummy.
She earned it by taking such good care
of the house.
He also bought a present for his son, Huckle.
Huckle was a very good helper today.

Mother's work is never done

Good Morning! Good Morning!
The sun is up! Everybody up!
Wash! Brush! Comb! Dress!

Get up! There is
a lot of work to be done!

Mummy cooked breakfast. Sally helped her serve it.

Daddy gave Mummy money to buy groceries.
Mummy gave Daddy a kiss as he hurried off to work.

Mummy and Sally and Harry washed the dishes
—and the kitchen floor.

They made the beds.

They cleaned the house.

They drove to the grocery store
to buy food and other things
that they needed at home.

Mummy made sandwiches for lunch.

A brush salesman came to the door
to sell brushes. Mummy didn't want
to buy any brushes.
My! He is trying very hard to sell
Mummy a brush of some kind, isn't he?

At last, the salesman left.
Mummy washed some dirty clothes.

Sally and Harry helped Mummy prepare supper.

Daddy came home from work and kissed everyone.

They sat down to supper. Daddy should know better than to try to take such a big bite.

After supper Mummy gave Sally and Harry a bath.

Daddy weighed himself on the scales. I think he has eaten too much.

Daddy read a story before bedtime.

He climbed up to kiss Sally goodnight.
Oh dear! I just KNEW he had eaten too much!

Good Night!

Are you all right, Daddy?

I don't think anyone will ever
sleep in that bunk bed again.
Do you?

Sally and Harry had to sleep
with Mummy. What would we
ever do if we didn't have mummies to do
things for us all day—and sometimes all
night? Good night! Sleep tight!

A voyage on a ship

Irish Pennant
cargo boom
cargo winch
the ship's painter
dock
KEEP OFF
NUTS
WATER
FUEL OIL
APPLES
EGGS
FRESH DAILY
BREAD
CHEESE
MAIL
MAIL

Captain Salty and his Crew are getting
their ship ready for a voyage.
The ship will carry passengers to visit
their friends in a faraway land
across the ocean.

14

At last the ship is loaded with
the food and other things they
will need on the long trip.
Here come the passengers!

They have all bought tickets
for the trip. They give the tickets to the
purser before they can go aboard the ship. NO PUSHING PLEASE!

light buoy

Toooooooooooot!
It is sailing time. A tiny tugboat pushes
the big ocean liner away from the pier.
Bon voyage! The big ship sails out of the harbour.

Soon it is crossing the wide ocean.
There is no land in sight.
Just look at all the things that
happen on an ocean-going ship!

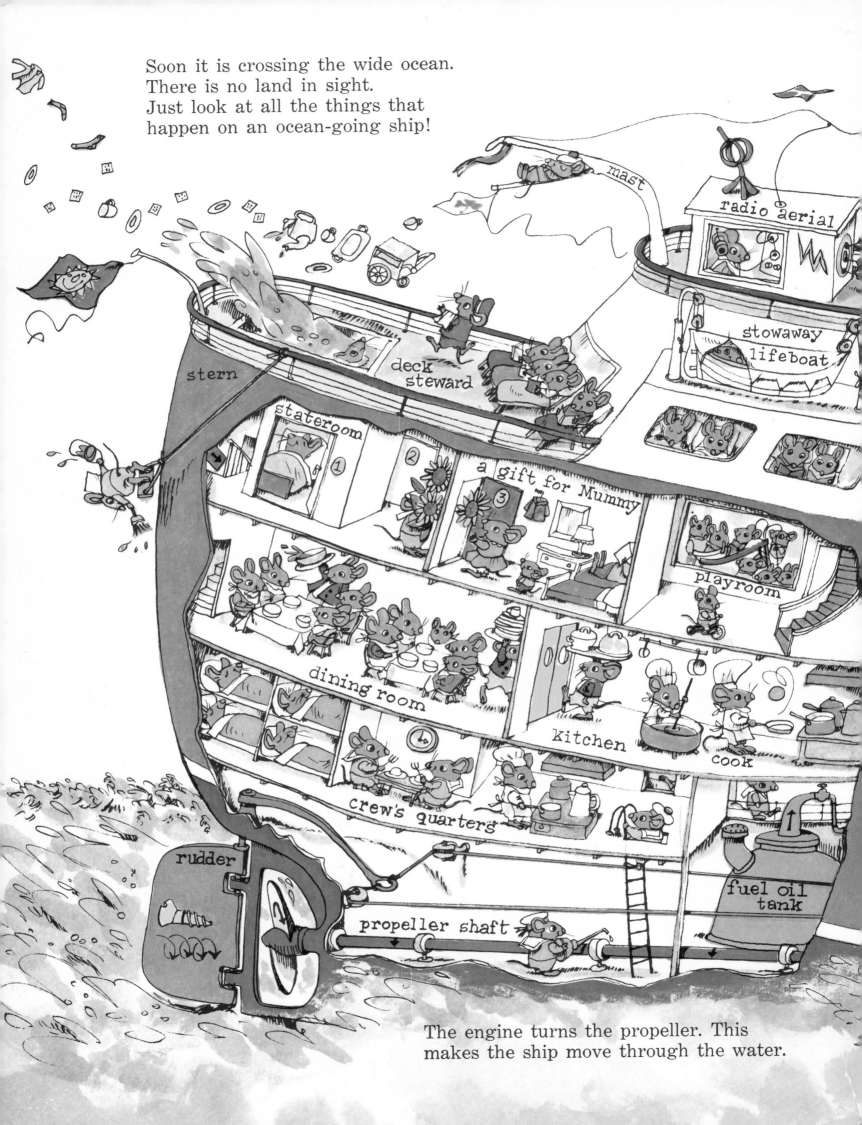

mast

radio aerial

stowaway
lifeboat

stern

deck
steward

stateroom

a gift for Mummy

playroom

dining room

kitchen

cook

crew's quarters

rudder

propeller shaft

fuel oil
tank

The engine turns the propeller. This
makes the ship move through the water.

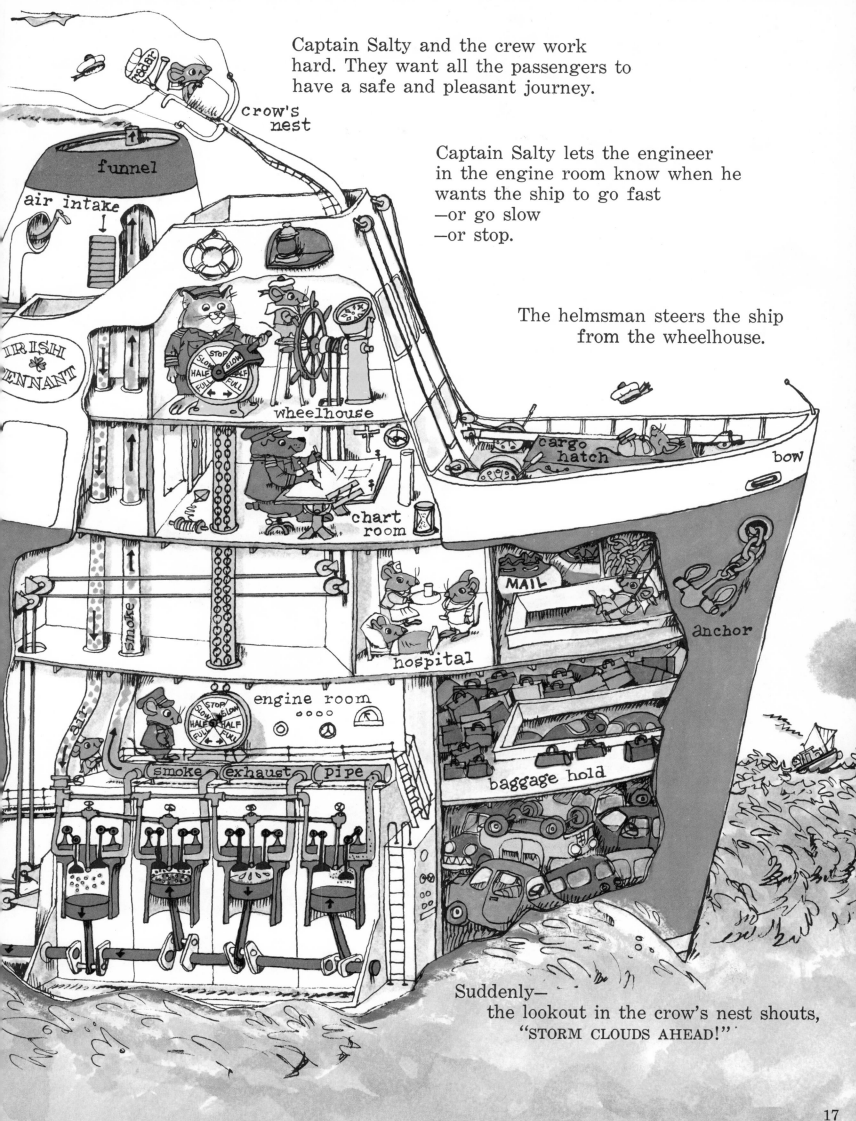

Captain Salty and the crew work hard. They want all the passengers to have a safe and pleasant journey.

Captain Salty lets the engineer in the engine room know when he wants the ship to go fast
—or go slow
—or stop.

The helmsman steers the ship from the wheelhouse.

crow's nest

funnel

air intake

IRISH PENNANT

radar

wheelhouse

STOP SLOW SLOW HALF FULL FULL

chart room

cargo hatch

bow

MAIL

anchor

hospital

smoke

air

engine room

STOP SLOW SLOW HALF HALF FULL FULL

smoke exhaust pipe

baggage hold

Suddenly—
    the lookout in the crow's nest shouts,
        "STORM CLOUDS AHEAD!"

17

The storm hits the ship with great fury!
The radio operator hears someone calling
on the radio.
"SOS! HELP! SAVE US! OUR BOAT IS SINKING!"

Look! There it is!
It's a small fishing boat in trouble!

"FULL SPEED AHEAD!"
roars Captain Salty.
My, the sea is rough!

LOWER THE LIFEBOAT!
Hurry! Hurry! The fishing boat is sinking!
Sailors Miff and Mo row to the rescue.

The boat sinks, but the fishermen are safe.

It's delicious!

LAND HO!!!

Back on board the liner, Captain Salty
gives a party to celebrate the rescue.
Will the storm never stop?

Then, just as suddenly as it started,
the storm is over and the sea is calm.
The ship continues on its journey.

Land ho! They have reached
the other side of the ocean!

Everyone thanks the captain and crew for such
an exciting voyage. Then they go ashore to visit friends.
Other people have been waiting to cross the ocean
to visit friends in Busytown. I wonder if their
voyage will be as exciting as this one was?

Sergeant Murphy of the Busytown Police Department

Policemen are working at all times to keep things safe and peaceful.
When Sergeant Murphy is sleeping, Policeman Louie is awake.
He will protect the townspeople from harm.

Good Morning!
Sleep Tight!

In the morning, Officer Louie goes home to bed and Sergeant Murphy gets up. Now Sergeant Murphy will watch out for everyone's safety.

At the Police Station the police chief tells Murphy to drive around town on his motorcycle. The chief can talk to Murphy over the radio if he has something important to tell him.

Keep everything peaceful!

First, Murphy saves Huckle from drowning in the fountain.

Then he has to stop two bad boys from fighting.
Look Murphy! There are two more!

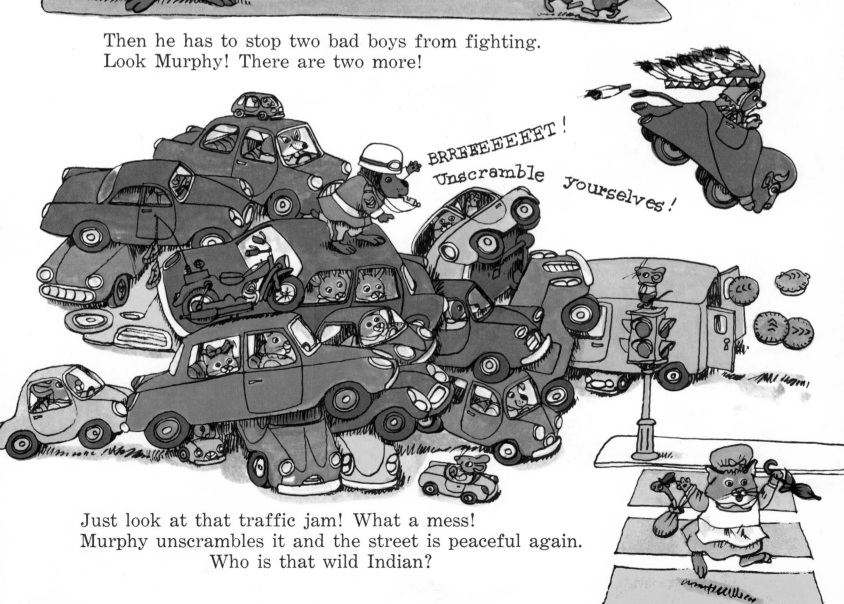

Just look at that traffic jam! What a mess!
Murphy unscrambles it and the street is peaceful again.
Who is that wild Indian?

O HO!
Wild Bill Hiccup
and his Buffalomobile!
He's speeding again!

He puts parking tickets on cars that are parked where they are not supposed to be.

Did you see that speeder hit Murphy's motorcycle? Chase him, Murphy!

Try to be good!

Murphy gives him a speeding ticket. For punishment he will not be allowed to drive his Buffalomobile for a few days. Let that be a lesson to you, Wild Bill Hiccup!

GROCERIES
I've been robbed!

Catch the thief!

Now—guess what?
Grocer Cat telephones the Police Station.
A robber has stolen some bananas from the grocery store.

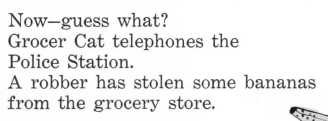

The chief of police calls Murphy over the radio.
"CATCH THE THIEF!" he says.

Look Murphy! There's the thief now!
It's Gorilla Bananas!

Murphy chases after him.
OOPS! His motorcycle slipped
on a banana peel. It is good
that he is wearing a crash helmet.

He has captured Bananas!

The paddy wagon comes to take Bananas to jail.
He will stay there until he learns that
it is wrong to steal things from others.

Nice work, Murphy!

It is time for Murphy to stop working.
Now he can go home for supper with his family.
Policeman Louie wakes up. He will keep
everything peaceful during the night.

In the middle of the night,
Louie hears a loud crying noise.
If the noise doesn't stop
it will wake up everyone in town.
Why, it is Bridget, Murphy's little girl!
WAKE UP, MURPHY! BRIDGET IS HUNGRY!

Murphy has to get up and warm
a bottle of milk for Bridget.
Bridget stops crying.

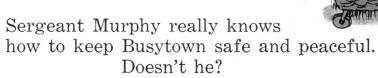

Sergeant Murphy really knows
how to keep Busytown safe and peaceful.
Doesn't he?

Firemen to the rescue

FIRE!
Mother Cat was ironing
one of Daddy's shirts.
The iron was too hot.
The shirt began to burn.
"FIRE!" she shouted.

Davy Dog went to the
fire-alarm Box. He pulled
the knob that sounded
the alarm at the fire station.

LOCATION OF
ALARM BOXES

Hurry!

Firemen are at the fire station
at all times. They have to be
ready to put fires out quickly.

As soon as the alarm rang,
they ran to their fire engines.
HURRY!

Clang! Clang! Clang!
The firemen rushed to the fire.
They raised the ladder on the ladder truck.
A fireman ran up the ladder to rescue Mummy.
"SAVE MY HUCKLE!" she screamed.

RESCUE-10

ALARM BOX

PUMPER ENGINE

CHIEF

Save Huckle too!

water hydrant

Water is used to put fires out.
The water runs through pipes under the street.
The firemen attached a hose between the
water hydrant and the pumper engine.
The pumper engine got water from the hydrant
and squirted it out through the hose nozzle.

But the ladder wasn't
long enough to reach Huckle
up in the playroom!
How will they ever save him?

"SAVE MY HUCKLE!" screamed Mummy Cat
as the firemen carried her down.

Smokey came running to the house.
He had a smoke mask so that
he would be able to breathe
in the smoke-filled house.

He also had
a special ladder.

He climbed up the
fire-truck ladder
as far as he could.
He reached up with
his special ladder
and hooked it over
the window sill. Then he
climbed up.
He just had to
rescue Huckle!

The playroom door was closed.
Smokey chopped it down with his axe.

He picked up Huckle—
and he jumped out the window!

PLOPP!
Sparky and Snozzle were ready
just in time to catch them
in the life net.
Daddy arrived just in time
to see Smokey save Huckle.

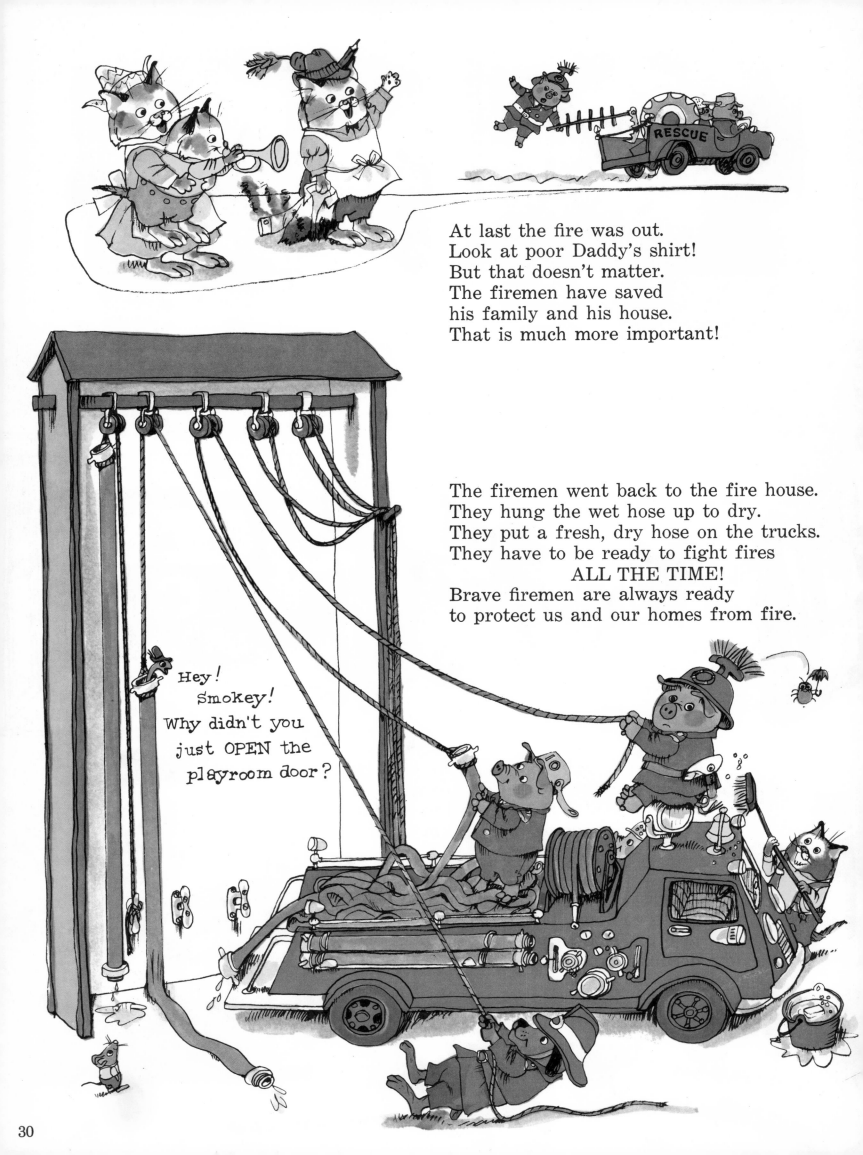

At last the fire was out.
Look at poor Daddy's shirt!
But that doesn't matter.
The firemen have saved
his family and his house.
That is much more important!

The firemen went back to the fire house.
They hung the wet hose up to dry.
They put a fresh, dry hose on the trucks.
They have to be ready to fight fires
ALL THE TIME!
Brave firemen are always ready
to protect us and our homes from fire.

Hey!
Smokey!
Why didn't you
just OPEN the
playroom door?

A visit to the hospital

Mummy took Abby to visit Doctor Lion.
He looked at her tonsils.
"Hmmmm. Very bad tonsils," he said.
"I shall have to take them out.
Meet me at the hospital tomorrow."

On the next day, Daddy drove them to the hospital.
Abby waved to the ambulance driver.
Ambulances bring people to hospitals
if they have to get there in a hurry.

Nurse Nelly was waiting for Abby.
Mummy had to go home, but she
promised to bring Abby a present
after the doctor had taken her
tonsils out.

Nurse Nelly took Abby up to the children's room.

Roger Dog was in the bed next to hers.
His tonsils were already out.
He was eating a big dish of ice cream.

Nurse Nelly put Abby on the bed.
She pulled a curtain around them.
No one could see what was going on.

Why, she was helping Abby
put on a nightgown!

Doctor Lion peeked into the room.
He told Nurse Nelly he was going
to put on his operating clothes.
He told Nurse Nelly to bring
Abby to the operating room.

Off to the operating room they went.
Doctor Lion was waiting there.
Everyone but the patient wears
a face mask in the operating room
so that germs won't spread.

Doctor Lion told Abby that she
was going to go to sleep.
He said she would stay asleep
until her tonsils were out.

Doctor Dog put a mask
over her nose and mouth.
She breathed in and out.
In an instant she was asleep.

When she woke up she found
herself back in the bed next
to Roger's. Her tonsils were all gone!
Her throat was sore, but it felt better
after she had some ice cream.

Whoooooeeee!
Abby saw her Mummy arriving
in the ambulance.
Abby thought her mother must be
in a hurry to see her.

She waited and waited
—but Mummy didn't come.
At last Doctor Lion came.
"Your Mother has brought you
a present," he said.
He took Abby for a ride
in a wheelchair.

"There is your present," he said.
"It is your new baby brother!
Your mother just gave birth to
him here in the hospital."
Then they all went to Mummy's
room in the hospital.
Daddy was there, too.

What a lucky girl she was!
She left her tonsils
at the hospital,
but she brought home
a lovely baby brother.

He looks like me, don't you think?

But remember! Very few children receive such
a nice present when they have their tonsils out!

The train trip

The Pig family is going on a train
to visit their cousins in a town far away.
They will travel all day and all night to get there.

Daddy buys train tickets
at the railway station.

Mummy buys books
and magazines to read.

A porter takes their bags
to the train.

This old train has a steam engine.
It is only going to make
a short trip to the next town.
The Pig family will ride
overnight on another train.

Their train has a sleeping car
with separate rooms for each family.
These rooms are called compartments.
At night, the seats will be made into beds.
Look! There is Huckle's family.

Food and water is brought to
the kitchen in the dining car.
The cook will cook their meals.
The waiter will serve them.

ALL ABOOOOOARD!
It is time to leave.
The train rolls out of the station.
The signal light tells the engineer
that there is a clear track ahead.
He doesn't want to bump into another train.

signal tower

Mailbags and heavy baggage
are put on the train.
Some of it will be delivered
to stations along the way.

The locomotive needs fuel oil
to make its motors go.
The motors turn the wheels so that
the train can roll along the railway track.

The switchman can
switch the train
from one track to another.
If he makes a mistake
the train won't go
to the right place.

The ticket collector takes the tickets. The tickets show that Daddy has paid for the trip.

In Huckle's compartment, the porter is getting the pillows and blankets ready for bedtime.

DINING CAR

MAIL

MAIL

It is time to eat dinner.
Cookie has already made the soup.
He is trying to toss the pancakes
from the side that is cooked
to the side that is not cooked.
You are not doing very well, Cookie!

The postman delivers a bag of mail to the railway station of a town they are passing through.

The watchman lowers the crossing
gates before a train crosses a road.
He doesn't want any cars to
bump into the train.
But Wild Bill Hiccup
just HAS to bump into something!

Oh dear!
The train has swerved and the
waiter has spilled the soup!

While they are eating,
the porter changes
their seats into beds.

After dinner, everyone gets ready for bed.

Clickety clack, clickety clack.
The train speeds on through the night.
The train crew won't go to sleep
until the trip is over.
Cookie is still trying to learn how to
toss pancakes. Keep trying, Cookie.

It is morning when they
arrive at their cousin's town.
Their cousins are at the
railway station to greet them.
I think they will have fun
on their visit. Don't you?

Wood
and how we use it

We couldn't live without trees.
We get wood from trees.
We use wood in many ways.
Let's see how we get our wood.

TIMBER!

The lumberjack cuts down the tree.

The branches are cut off the tree trunk.

The tree trunk is sawed into logs.

tree trunk

a seed

a one year old tree

This tree is almost 100 years old and is ready to be cut down

log

The logs are put in a river to float downstream.

The forest ranger watches out
for fires. A forest fire
could burn down a whole forest.

Some trees are left standing.
Seeds from these trees
will fall to the ground.
New trees will grow in place of
the old ones that have been cut down.

The foresters also
scatter seeds from helicopters.

Loggers ride the logs down the river.
They try to keep the logs from getting jammed.
Oh dear! The logs are jammed!
Unscramble that log jam, loggers!

Good work, loggers!
You broke up the log jam.
Now the logs can float to
the sawmill and be sawed into boards.

TOM SAWYER'S SAWMILL

Water falling over
a water wheel makes
all the machinery work.

timber

timberyard

SAWDUST THE CARPENTER

BOAT BUILDER

FURNITURE

The logs are
sawed into
rough boards.

The rough wood is sawed
into boards of different sizes.

scrap timber

FOOLSCAP
PAPER CO.

straddle
truck

This timber is stacked
in the timberyard to dry.
Many kinds of workers come to buy the
timber they need for building things.
Daddy Pig has bought some timber
to build a bookcase.

The paper makers use scraps
of wood to make paper.

FOOLSCAP
PAPER
COMPANY

chipper

digester

chemicals

beater

mixer

blower

Wet wood pulp moves onto a wire screen belt.
Water is removed by rollers and dryers.

dry end | drying | paper making machine | wire screen | wet end | wet wood pulp

a finished
roll of paper

ABC PRINTERS

Some paper is used to make bags and boxes.
Some is for making books.
The paper used in this book was taken
to the printing shop where books are made.
The printer put the words
and pictures on the pages.

The boat builder uses curved
pieces of wood to make boats.

BOAT BUILDER

FURNITURE MAKER

lathe

jig saw

FURNITURE

The furniture maker makes beds and chests and chairs.

SAWDUST THE CARPENTER

Carpenters have a custom of nailing a tree branch to the roof of a new house.

Some trees give us fruit.

POLLY JAN

MA PA

D.S. D.C.

ICE CREAM

NEWS
GREAT Plumbing and Heating at the Raton house. More later.

Trees shade us from the hot sun.

Harry is planting an apple seed.
An apple tree will grow from the seed.
It will take a long time.
Someday YOU might like to plant a tree.

47

Digging COAL to make electricity work for us

steam boiler

FRESH AIR ENTER HERE

STOP GO

Pick! Pick! Pick! Dig! Dig! Dig! The miners dig coal out of the coal mine under the ground.

Water seeps into the mine, and has to be pumped out.

Lifts raise and lower the miners and coal cars.

After the coal is dug out, wooden props are needed to hold up the roof.

coal

The miners use picks and drills to break the coal into small pieces.

The seeping water collects in the sump.

sump

BURIED SUNLIGHT COAL MINE

THE TIPPLE

COAL

COAL

DIANE

Many years ago, sunlight poured down
on the plants and trees
and helped them to grow.
When these plants and trees died,
they sank into the ground.
Gradually they were changed into coal.

The coal is brought up out
of the mine to the tipple.
Then it is loaded into
railway coal cars.

Miners need fresh air.
A fan blows out the stale air
and fresh air rushes in.

The miners blast the
hard, black coal
with explosives.

EXPLOSIVE

stale air
leaves this way

The loader loads coal
into small coal cars.

TO THE
TIPPLE

loader

By burning coal, we are able to make electricity work for us.
The electricity lights our homes.
That is why we call coal "buried sunlight."
There is electricity in everything. But it is not useful to us
until it is moving. Coal helps to make electricity move.

A train brings
the coal to the
electric power plant.

The coal is burned in the boiler
to heat water. The heat turns the
water into steam. The boiler works
like a tea kettle.

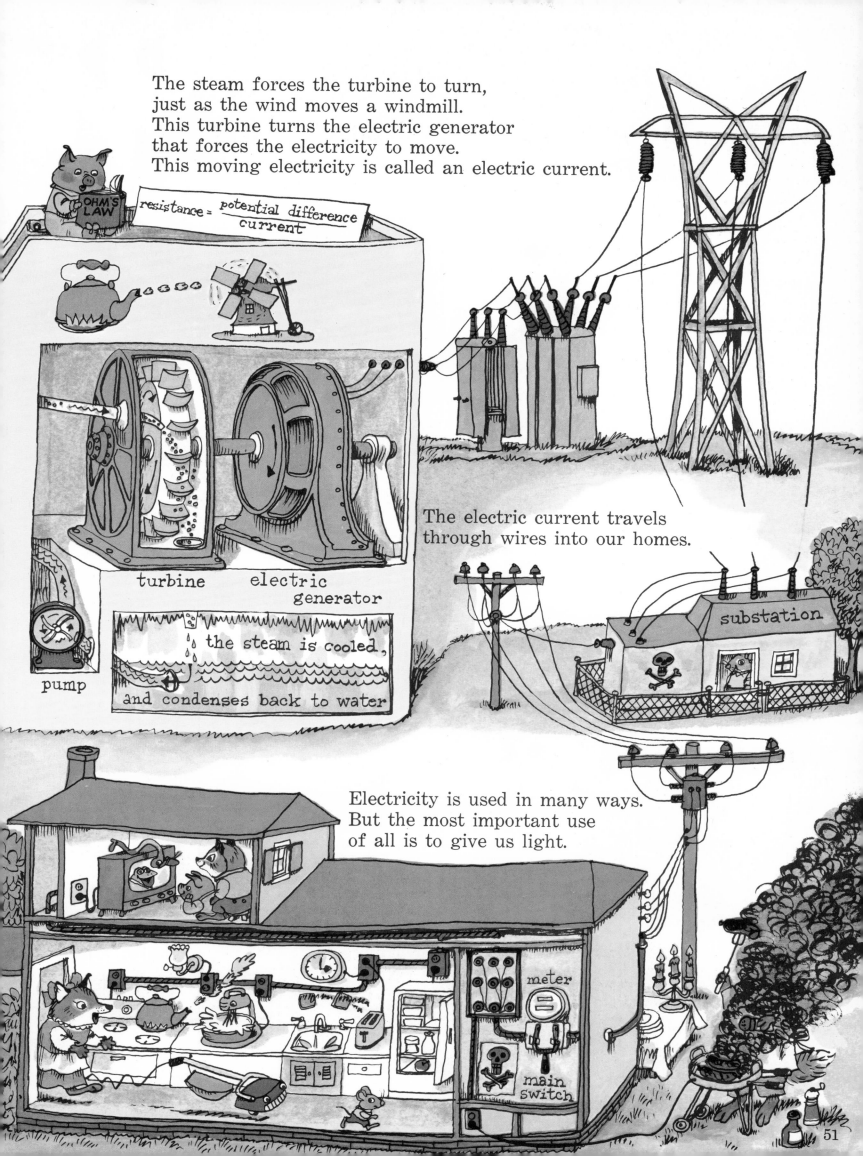

The steam forces the turbine to turn,
just as the wind moves a windmill.
This turbine turns the electric generator
that forces the electricity to move.
This moving electricity is called an electric current.

OHM'S LAW

resistance = potential difference / current

turbine   electric generator

the steam is cooled,
and condenses back to water

pump

The electric current travels
through wires into our homes.

substation

Electricity is used in many ways.
But the most important use
of all is to give us light.

meter

main switch

51

Building a new road

Good roads are very important to all of us.
Doctors need them to visit patients.
Firemen need them to go to fires.
We all need them to visit one another.
The road between Busytown and Workville
was bumpy and crooked and very dusty—

—except when it rained!
Then the dirt turned to mud and everyone got stuck.

The mayors of the two towns went to the road engineer
and told him that they wanted to have a new road.
The townspeople had agreed to pay the road engineer
and his workers to build the new road.

Get rid of those bumps!
Make this road flat and straight, Bugdozer!

OK, Chief!

surveying instrument

ROAD PLANS

BUMP

The surveyor used his instruments to make sure that the road would be straight.

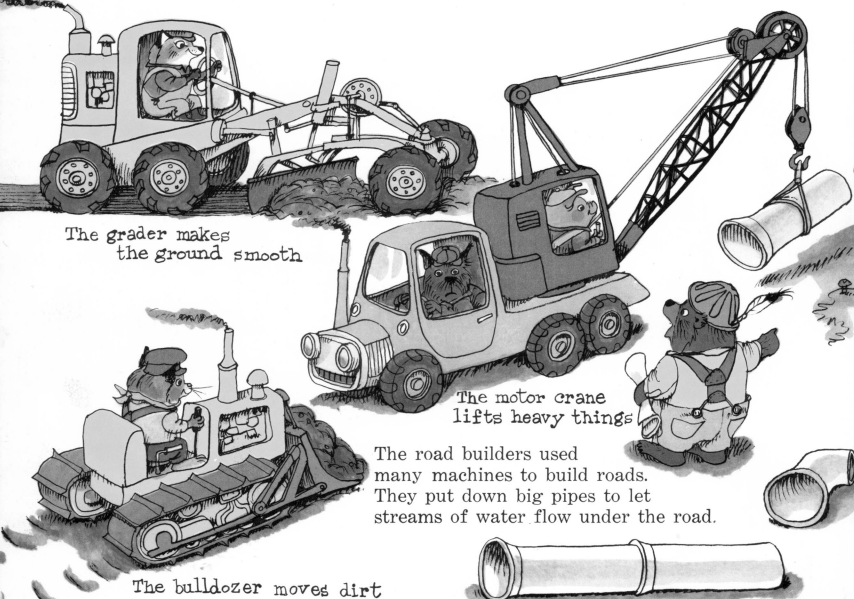

The grader makes the ground smooth

The motor crane lifts heavy things

The road builders used many machines to build roads. They put down big pipes to let streams of water flow under the road.

The bulldozer moves dirt

The surveyor's helpers used stakes and
string to show where the road was to go.

water drainage ditch

tractor
shovel

dump
truck

ditch digger

At last the roadbed was
straight and smooth.
But it needed a hard top
so that there would be no dust or mud.

Big rocks were put into the rock crusher
to be crushed into smaller stones.

A stone spreader spread the stones
evenly over the roadbed.

A truck squirted sticky asphalt oil
on the stones to make them stick together.

The stone cutter shapes
the stones so that they
will fit next to each other

The asphalt mixer made hot, sticky asphalt.

The asphalt was poured into
the level finisher, which
spread it out flat on the road.

A heavy roller
pressed down the asphalt
to make it smooth and hard.

A GOOD ROAD

How am I doing, Chief?

The road was built high in the middle
so that rain water would roll off
into ditches at the sides.

57

Street lights were put up so that drivers could see the road clearly at night.

FIREFLY LIGHTING COMPANY

electric cable

SNACK BAR

EAT

PETROL

petrol pump

PETROL & OIL

DIVIDING LINE PAINTER

petrol storage tank

GARDENER

OIL OIL OIL OIL OIL OIL

All right you two fellows! Stop talking and finish covering up that underground storage tank!

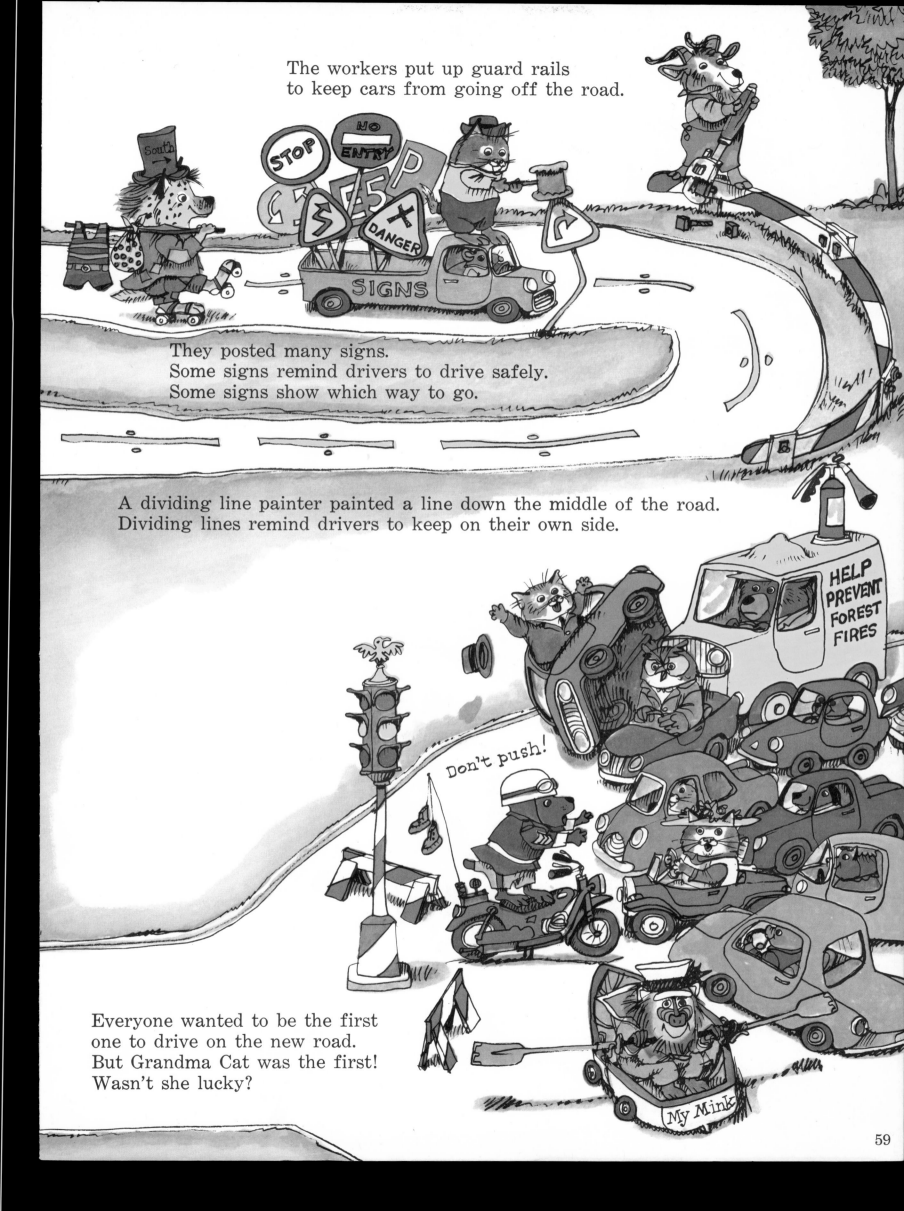

The workers put up guard rails
to keep cars from going off the road.

They posted many signs.
Some signs remind drivers to drive safely.
Some signs show which way to go.

A dividing line painter painted a line down the middle of the road.
Dividing lines remind drivers to keep on their own side.

Don't push!

Everyone wanted to be the first
one to drive on the new road.
But Grandma Cat was the first!
Wasn't she lucky?

Water

We all need water. Nothing
on earth can live without it.
Even though we can't see it,
there is a lot of water in the air.
Sometimes it falls to earth as rain or snow.
Then we can see it and feel it.

Now, let's see how we can make
water work for us.

stream

water reservoir

water intake

dam

a picnic

ELECTRIC POWER STATION

ELECTRIC GENERATOR

CROSS SECTION OF DAM

dam

A dam has been built across the
river valley to hold the water back.
After the water has been used
in the electric power plant, it flows
as a river down to the sea.

The wind turns the whirling
vanes on the windmill.
This causes buckets to lift water
to feed the thirsty plants in the
farm field up above the river.

Water lies in pools underground
and can be pumped up for use.

river

The river water must be made clean
and pure, so that it will be safe to drink.
Water is pumped into the waterworks.

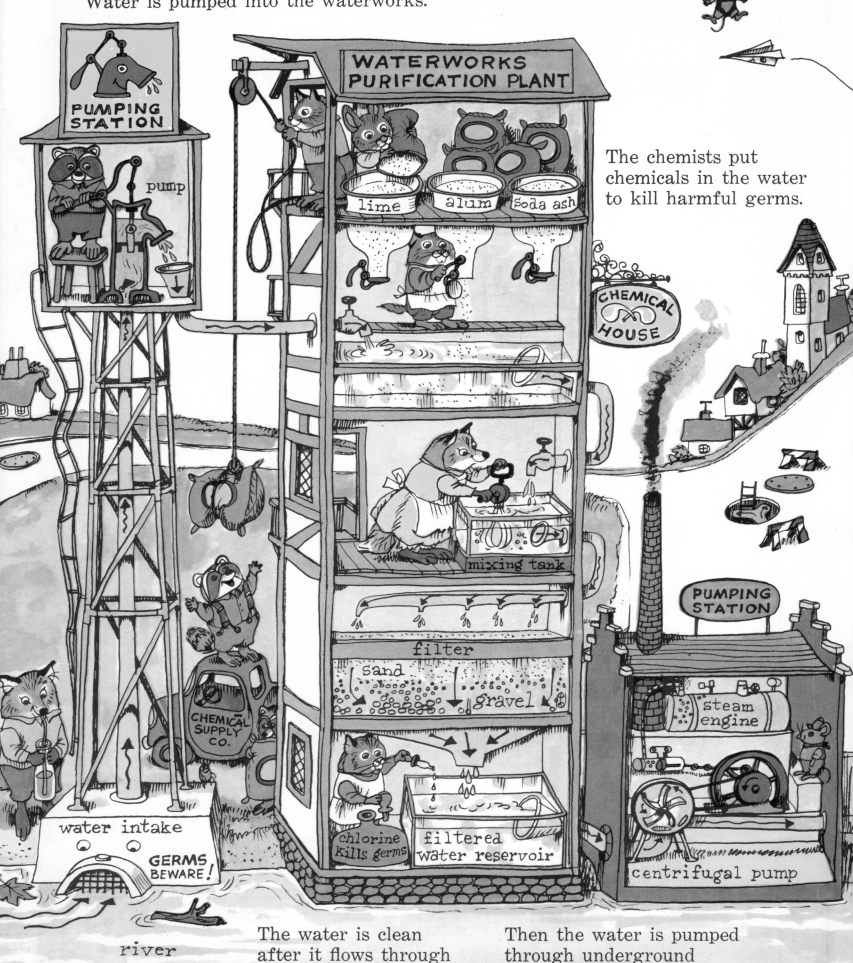

PUMPING STATION

pump

WATERWORKS
PURIFICATION PLANT

lime   alum   soda ash

The chemists put
chemicals in the water
to kill harmful germs.

CHEMICAL
HOUSE

mixing tank

CHEMICAL
SUPPLY
CO.

PUMPING
STATION

filter

sand   gravel

steam
engine

water intake

GERMS
BEWARE!

chlorine
kills germs

filtered
water reservoir

centrifugal pump

The water is clean
after it flows through
the waterworks.

Then the water is pumped
through underground
pipes to everyone.

river

river bank